COPING WITH FOSTER CARE

Jeanne Nagle

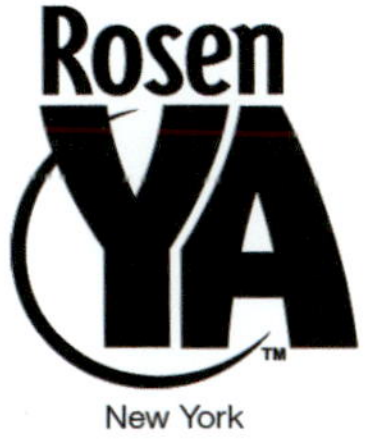

New York

For James F. Nagle
You are my sunshine. Thanks for everything, Dad.

Published in 2020 by The Rosen Publishing Group, Inc.
29 East 21st Street, New York, NY 10010

First Edition

Library of Congress Cataloging-in-Publication Data

Names: Nagle, Jeanne, author.
Title: Coping with foster care / Jeanne Nagle.
Description: First edition. | New York : Rosen Publishing, 2020. | Series: Coping | Includes bibliographical references and index.
Identifiers: LCCN 2019011126 | ISBN 9781725341234 (library binding) | ISBN 9781725341227 (paperback)
Subjects: LCSH: Foster home care—United States. | Foster children—Services for—United States.
Classification: LCC HV881 .N24 2020 | DDC 362.73/30973—dc23
LC record available at https://lccn.loc.gov/2019011126

Manufactured in the United States of America

Some of the images in this book illustrate individuals who are models. The depictions do not imply actual situations or events.

On the cover: Although coping methods may sometimes be hard to come by, it's important to remember that no one faces being in foster care alone.

CONTENTS

INTRODUCTION

Comedian Tiffany Haddish entered the foster care system when she was thirteen. She and her siblings were placed in separate foster homes after their mother was diagnosed with a mental illness and became abusive. After two years of living in other people's homes, Haddish and her siblings were sent to live with their grandmother in what is known as kinship care.

Haddish dealt with being in foster care by becoming a class clown, which frequently got her in trouble. The social worker assigned to her case gave her the option of going to therapy or attending a comedy camp at the Los Angeles Laugh Factory. She chose camp. Attending taught her to communicate and channel her nervous energy into something productive. These days Haddish shows up at the camp to mentor kids, many of whom are in the same boat she once was.

Brandon became a foster child around age eight. He spent time in ten temporary foster locations, including three years in a detention center when he was a teenager. He hadn't done anything wrong. At the time, the detention center was the only place the system could find to house an older child like him.

Once he turned seventeen, Brandon moved out of the foster care system. He dedicated himself

In interviews, actress and comedian Tiffany Haddish has been very upfront about her time in foster care, from the highs to the lows and everything in between.

to getting an education, becoming the first member of his birth family to graduate from high school and also the first to graduate from college. "I am a living testament that just because you were in foster care does not mean you cannot be somebody," he said in a video posted on Soulpancake in 2018.

Tony had been placed in the foster care system at a young age, taken out of his home because of neglect. He had been placed for adoption by the time he turned four. Even though he wasn't officially in the system for long, Tony believes the experience deeply affected him. His health suffered because of “failure to thrive,” meaning he didn’t grow and gain weight at a normal rate because he had not been properly fed and cared for as an infant. He had abandonment issues, constantly asking his adopted mother for reassurance that she would not give up on him as his birth mother had.

Eventually, thanks to the love and support of his new mother, Tony got through the rough spots and emerged as a healthy, happy adult. He has worked for years as a sportswriter, taking after his journalist mom. As a parent himself now, he says he works hard to let his daughter know he will always be there for her.

These are only three examples of children who, through no fault of their own, were placed in the United States foster care system. Each had a rough time dealing with life as a foster child. But as the stories of Tiffany, Brandon, and Tony attest, there are things foster kids can do, as well as available resources and people willing to get involved, that can help them cope with being in foster care.

CHAPTER ONE

What Foster Care Is and Isn't

Simply put, foster care is one of the ways society has chosen to take care of children when their birth parents cannot or do not. This is accomplished by legally removing kids from situations that may be physically or emotionally harmful and placing them somewhere that is supposed to be safer. The foster care system is meant to be temporary, with the ultimate goal of finding a permanent place where the child can be well cared for and, ultimately, loved.

Yet there really isn't anything simple about foster care. From the way it is administered to the toll it takes on the children who enter the system, as well as their foster and birth families, foster care is a complex practice filled with emotion.

The Roots of Foster Care

Foster care in the United States dates back to the seventeenth century, before there even was a United States. British settlements and colonies in the New World adopted a version of England's "poor laws," which gave orphans and children from poor families to other people as servants. Essentially, these children were made to work in exchange for a place to live until they were old enough to strike out on their own. Some people have likened the system to slavery.

In the 1800s, a new wrinkle was added to this arrangement with the formation of the Children's Aid Society. Led by a minister named Charles Loring Brace, the organization saw to it that hundreds of thousands of children living in orphanages or on the streets of New York City were sent to work for families in the rural Midwest. These moves were designed to protect children from life on the street or the loneliness and abuse found in many orphanages. This type of early foster care program operated under the belief that hard work, performed under the direction of caretakers in a safer and healthier environment, would best prepare these children for their lives as independent adults. Unfortunately, there were many cases of abuse under this system. Often caregivers were more inclined to view the

Youngsters, waiting outside the Children's Aid Society office In New York City, prepare to board one of Charles Loring Brace's "orphan trains."

children they agreed to foster as servants rather than loved members of the family. Even those who created and ran the system had ulterior motives. In addition to helping vulnerable children, they had an eye toward stabilizing the nation's economy by sending cheap labor to add to a workforce in the burgeoning Midwest.

The Society for the Prevention of Cruelty to Children (SPCC) was formed to address issues of

This nineteenth-century illustration shows children being put under the care of the SPCC after being caught begging. This situation might raise suspicions of homelessness, neglect, and abuse.

child abuse in both foster and birth families, in much the same way the Society for the Prevention of Cruelty to Animals (SPCA) sought to stop instances of animal abuse. SPCC chapters across the country were given the power to remove children from dangerous situations and place them elsewhere.

In 1912, the federal government got involved in child welfare with the formation of the Children's Bureau, which was created to protect the physical and emotional health and well-being of children across the country. In addition to conducting investigations and issuing reports, the bureau was charged with distributing federal money to individual states for efforts to control child welfare matters within their own borders. This setup, with federal oversight and funding but individual state control and responsibility, is still the norm today.

Reasons for Foster Care

The foster care system in the United States largely grew out of a desire by individuals who, despite some ulterior motives, wanted to make life better for homeless and poverty-stricken youth, as well as children who had been orphaned. Caring for vulnerable children is still the main concept that

Foster Care Around the World

There are differences among various nations around the world with regard to how foster care systems are set up and funded. In developing countries with struggling economies, fostering is done informally, if at all. Developed countries generally have formal fostering programs with some kind of government oversight. In North America, Canadian provinces are in charge of foster care programs, just as individual states are in the United States. However, whereas the US federal government oversees and funds the states' child protection efforts, the provinces run their operations completely on their own, without assistance or interference from the federal government in Ottawa.

Other differences include how countries approach the practice of fostering. Some countries, such as Australia and Sweden, focus more on working out issues with the entire family while the child stays in the home. Canada and the United States, however, share a foster care philosophy that puts the safety of the child above all else, often resulting in children being removed, at least temporarily, from the birth home while issues are resolved.

drives foster care today. However, the reasons how and why kids enter the system have shifted or, more accurately, expanded. These days, rather than picked up off the streets, foster children are more likely to have been taken from a bad situation at a home where they lived under the care of at least one parent or adult caregiver.

Neglect and Abandonment

Neglect is among the top reasons children may be removed from their home and placed in foster care. The case can be made for neglect if a child does not receive the basic necessities of life, such as adequate food and water, or if he or she is forced to live in conditions that are poor enough to be considered unsanitary or otherwise dangerous to health and well-being. Leaving young children alone and unsupervised for an extended period of time also counts as neglect. Even if a parent is present in the home but incapacitated—for instance, under the influence of drugs or alcohol—the courts may find the adult guilty of neglect.

Abandonment is closely related to neglect. Leaving a child alone or with someone else without any intention of coming back and taking care of him or her is abandonment. So is a parent leaving the family home because of divorce or some other

Neglect can leave children feeling alone and cut off from others. These feelings make them more vulnerable to negative influences or more open to making bad decisions.

reason, and consequently not having contact with the child for a long period of time.

Forms of Abuse

Evidence of abuse is another major concern when considering whether or not a child should be placed in foster care. Physical maltreatment is probably the first type of abuse that springs to mind when considering foster care placement. Children who are beaten or assaulted in some way that causes bodily harm are considered victims of physical abuse. Continually yelling and screaming at children, and insulting them or threatening them, are forms of emotional abuse. These are actions that injure a kid's emotional well-being or sense of self-worth. Because it makes children feel as if they do not matter enough to be kept clean or well-fed, neglect can also be considered a form of emotional abuse.

Sexual abuse is another reason that may cause a child to be

The Role of Caseworkers

Child welfare caseworkers are key participants in the foster care process, from start to finish. Employees of state or local government social services agencies, namely Child Protective Services (CPS), are caseworkers who receive reports of abuse or neglect. Through assessments and investigations, they work to determine whether or not maltreatment actually happened. If it has, they present their findings to a child welfare judge, who decides whether or not to remove a child from his or her birth home.

Once a child has entered the foster care system, caseworkers help birth parents develop a plan to bring the family back together. They are also supposed to make themselves available to foster parents and children, to help resolve issues and answer questions. Child welfare caseworkers are on the job until foster kids have entered into a permanent living situation, whether that is back with their birth parents, adopted by another family, or moving on to independent living as a legal adult.

removed from his or her home and placed in foster care. Experts believe that both physical and sexual abuse often cause emotional harm to a child.

Incapacity and Voluntary Placement

Sometimes the adult in a single-parent household becomes incapacitated, meaning certain circumstances make it so that he or she is no longer able to take care of the child. Poor health, particularly if the person has to be hospitalized for any length of time, can lead to a parent's inability to look after a child. In this instance, the authorities will try to contact a relative to temporarily care for children under the age of eighteen. Until someone can be found, children of a sick parent may be temporarily placed in some kind of foster care facility. The same is often true if a parent or guardian is sent to jail or is required to enter a rehabilitation facility for drug addiction.

The common thread is that the parent is incapacitated and unable to care for his or her children at home. Taking this a step further, one could think of death as the ultimate incapacitation. Children whose parents have died, also known as orphans, used to be placed in institutions known as orphanages, and still are in other parts of the world. In the United States, however, foster care takes the place of orphanages. As with other forms

Leaving children in the care of relatives, including grandparents, aunts, or uncles, is the preferred placement method of virtually every foster care agency.

of incapacitation, attempts are made to find a living relative to take care of children whose parents have died. Foster care may only be a temporary situation in this case, unless a relative who is able and willing to take in the children cannot be found.

Another path leading to foster care involves a parent or parents voluntarily giving up their parental rights to children. This means they legally agree to no longer have a say in decisions involving how their child is raised. Children whose parents give up their rights may be placed for adoption, but first they may enter foster care until adoptive parents are found. There is no typical reason why a parent would willingly give up their children. Each parent has his or her reasons for taking such a drastic step. Thankfully, for all involved, this situation is much less common than the other reasons for why kids are placed in foster care.

Children in the System

The effects of foster care are far-reaching. Several people may be involved for each and every foster care case, including siblings and other relatives, group-home staff, child welfare social workers and other government employees, police officers, lawyers, and judges. But the main people involved in foster care placement are, of course, the children who are placed in the system. Foster children are considered wards of the state, meaning state welfare agencies or courts have legal custody of them.

Those who enter the foster care system are usually referred to as foster children, but the truth of the matter is, not all foster kids are actually children. They can range in age from newborns to teens up

A social worker helps homeless teens with their homework. Social workers are part of a multiperson network of individuals meant to help kids navigate the foster care system.

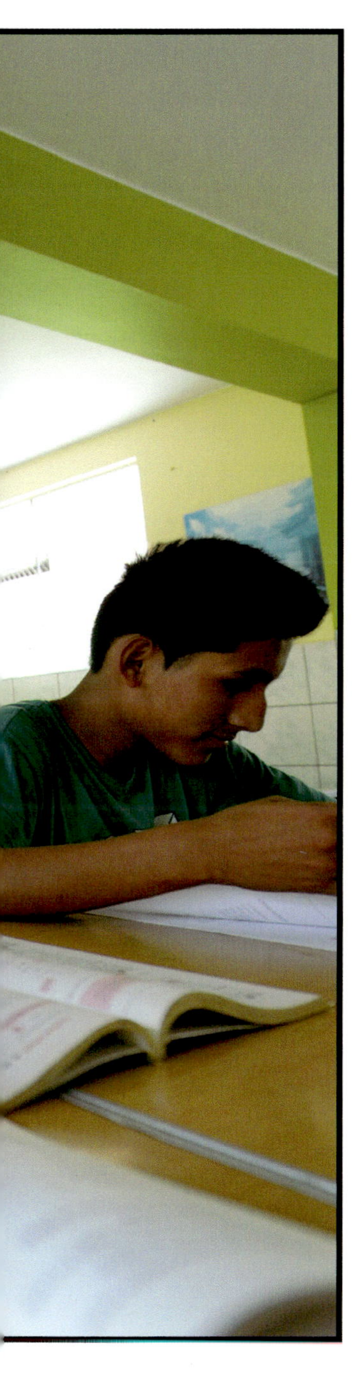

to the age of eighteen (or twenty-one in some states). Data from the US Department of Health and Human Services indicates that, since 2010, the number of kids in the US foster care system each year has hovered around four hundred thousand. The same data shows that on average, kids stay in foster care for about a year, at which time they may either be reunified with their birth families or adopted. Keep in mind, however, that there are children who stay in the system longer than a year. Some remain in foster care until they "age out," meaning they turn eighteen years old (or twenty-one) and leave the system because they are considered adults.

Roughly half of foster children and teens are reunited with their families in any given year. In order for reunification to happen, birth parents must undergo a multistep process designed to help them correct the behavior and circumstances that led to foster care placement. This may include seeking drug and alcohol rehabilitation, taking anger management classes, receiving mental health counseling, or securing a clean, safe place to live. Almost always there is some kind of parenting class involved.

The process, which is aimed at proving that a parent is able and willing to care for the child, is referred to as a case plan. Alternative names are treatment plan or reunification plan. Birth parents are given a time limit in which to complete the steps of the plan, usually anywhere from twelve to fifteen months. Failure to stick to or complete the plan may result in parental rights being terminated, and the child being available for adoption.

CHAPTER TWO

How the System Works

One of the frustrations children and teens might feel when they enter into the foster care system is a lack of control over what is happening. First, they struggle through a bad home situation that is not of their own making; then they are taken away, often with no notice. They are placed in a new living situation, with strangers, and no one even asks if they want to leave or what type of placement they might prefer. Is it any wonder that feelings of being insignificant and powerless might linger?

Foster kids may not feel as if they have much say in the matter, but there is something they can do to gain a measure of control. Knowing where they are in the foster care process should at least help children feel as if they are in the loop and can help prepare them for the next steps. Therefore,

Feeling upset and powerless are very real concerns for children and teens who find themselves in the foster care system.

learning all they can about the way the foster care system operates can be tremendously empowering.

Getting Clued In

Virtually every case of foster care placement begins after a state's child welfare organizations become aware that a child is being mistreated or is in danger at home. Tips and reports of suspected abuse or neglect are made to CPS, which is a local or community-wide division within each state's system of child welfare and social services agencies. These reports are generally made by phone, either directly to a CPS office or via a hotline set up specifically for this purpose. Reports should include as much information as possible about the child, his or her parents, and the living situation in the family home. A description of the specific incident that sparked the report is also important.

Any number of people can voluntarily file a report with CPS, including neighbors, relatives, a friend's parent, or basically any adult who is caring and observant. In fact, some states have laws that make reporting suspected cases of child maltreatment mandatory. Even in states where reporting by everyone in the general public is not mandatory, there are certain professionals who are required to file a report. These include teachers, childcare workers, medical professionals, police officers, first responders, social workers, and members of the clergy. Mandated reporters face fines and jail time if they do not report suspected child abuse or neglect.

Initial reports are treated as if they are suspected cases of child abuse or neglect. Child

A CPS caseworker takes notes at her desk in Virginia. Documenting whether or not child mistreatment has taken place is only part of a caseworker's job.

welfare caseworkers review these reports to determine if there is enough evidence to justify an investigation. In most states, a juvenile or family court judge issues a court order to begin an investigation, based on CPS filing a petition on the child's behalf. Caseworkers have to take all reports they receive seriously.

Screened in, Screened Out

Determining whether or not a report should be fully investigated is part of a process known as screening. If, after reviewing a report of maltreatment, the caseworker determines that the evidence points toward possible abuse or neglect, the report is "screened in," and an investigation is formally opened. A child welfare investigation is a matter of public record, with state CPS offices keeping a "central registry" database containing investigation materials.

Reports can be "screened out," or set aside, if they do not contain enough evidence that maltreatment has occurred, or what the reporter has witnessed or uncovered is not considered true abuse or neglect in his or her state. For instance, a parent spanking a child is considered to be reasonable discipline, not abuse. From a legal standpoint, the difference seems to be the way in which a child is struck—open palm versus closed fist—and whether or not the intent is to punish or harm.

Caseworkers do not open an investigation for screened-out reports, but that does not mean they necessarily ignore the concerns of the reporter. They may refer the person making the report to a community resource or organization they feel is

Help in All Its Forms

A growing trend among CPS offices is to use an approach known as differential response, which offers caseworkers more than one option—opening a formal investigation—regarding screened-in reports.

Caseworkers interview as many household members as possible after they receive a report of potential abuse or neglect. How the family acts together can give them important clues.

In these cases, a risk assessment is performed, based on information in the report that determines how much risk there is to the child's safety. If the risk is determined to be high, an investigation is opened. If the risk is low to moderate, however, caseworkers have the option of conducting an off-the-record family assessment. The caseworker looks into the home life of a family against whom a report has been made, to figure out if there are any problem areas that could be smoothed over by community-based assistance, such as counseling or help finding suitable housing.

Results of this informal investigation are not recorded in the agency's central registry of reported maltreatment cases. The main goal of differential response is to help families avoid true cases of neglect or abuse by heading trouble spots off at the pass.

better equipped to handle the situation as reported. These include places that offer a family help to keep abuse or neglect from happening, such as family counseling.

Getting the Fuller Picture

In order to determine if maltreatment actually has occurred, CPS caseworkers must open an investigation. The agency investigates possible cases of maltreatment by parents, members of a child's family, or another known caregiver acting in place of a parent. Law enforcement is typically only called in when a child is mistreated by someone outside the family or someone other than an immediate caregiver.

Interviewing is a crucial part of a CPS investigation. People whom a caseworker might talk to include the parents and other adults who have regular contact with the child in question, such as teachers, doctors, childcare workers, or even babysitters. Teachers and childcare workers would be able to talk about any changes of behavior in a child who may have been abused. Also, the child may feel safe around these people and may confide in them regarding problems at home. Doctors and other medical professionals would be able to talk about any signs of physical abuse, such as bruises or broken bones. As mandated reporters, these people may have already called in a report about a particular family. If not, their testimony could help confirm or deny abuse claims by another party. Finally, a caseworker may talk face-to-face with the child.

An official CPS investigation comes to one of only two conclusions. If no definite evidence of maltreatment exists, then the report is considered unsubstantiated. Reports that are substantiated by

Injuries, especially if they happen often, may be a sign of physical abuse. Doctors and teachers need to be aware of such signs and file a report if necessary.

evidence uncovered during an investigation sets the stage for further action to keep the child safe. In substantiated cases of abuse or neglect, where the risk of further harm coming to the child is thought to be moderate or high, that child and any others living in the family home are likely to be removed and placed into the foster care system. A juvenile or family court judge has the final say regarding whether or not maltreatment has occurred.

Finding a Safe Place for Kids to Land

"Placement" is the foster care term for the process of finding a place for children to live when they are removed from their homes. Within the United States, there are three common types of placements. Children and teens may be placed with relatives, with foster families, or in a group home setting. Placement with relatives or a foster family are typically recommended over group homes, due in large part to the fact that private-home settings are more familiar to children than group homes.

Whenever possible, caseworkers search for a relative, such as a grandparent or aunt/uncle, who is willing and able to foster children in need. This type of placement is referred to as kinship care, because relatives are kin, meaning people who are related. Instead of just sending a child or teen to live with a relative temporarily, until parents can "get their act together," kinship care is a formal arrangement between the state and the relative. It comes with foster care training and payments made to the caregiver to help support the foster child. A similar type of setting is known as a non-relative kinship placement. This is where foster children live with someone they know and trust, even if they are not related.

The next best option, in the eyes of CPS, is placement with a foster family in a private home setting. CPS claims that attempts are made to keep some things in the foster child's life the same when making a placement. For instance, whenever possible, children and teens are placed in a foster home that will allow them to attend the same school as when they were in their birth home. Unfortunately, this can be difficult to accomplish, since there is not always a foster home available that would make a good match. As with caregivers in kinship care, foster parents are trained and compensated, which means paid, to cover the child's expenses.

Group foster homes are exactly what the name says—places that temporarily house and look after groups of six or more foster children and teens at a time. Instead of relatives or foster parents, group homes are staffed with people hired by the organization running it. Group homes are licensed by individual states. Obviously, this type of setting cannot offer the same home-like

It's lunchtime at the Children's Village home in New York. The trend in foster care is to place kids in private homes and use group homes only when absolutely necessary.

function or "feel" as placement with a relative or foster family. Therefore, they may not be as good at helping foster kids feel safe and secure. Several studies suggest that further abuse and maltreatment is more likely to occur in a group setting than in other types of placement. According to a 2017 report on foster care issued by the Brookings Institution in Washington, DC, group foster homes are widely "considered an option of last resort," meaning all other options for placement should be considered before placing children or, more likely, teens, in a group foster home. Social workers tend to use group homes to place kids first entering the system, until relatives can be located or a traditional foster home can be found. A shortage of suitable, available private foster caregivers may also make group home placement necessary.

Plan of Attack

Once a child has been placed in foster care, the goal becomes finding a way to keep him or her safe on a long-term basis. Birth parents are given an opportunity to make their family whole again by working with CPS to put together a permanency plan. This is a formal "to do" list for birth parents. A permanency plan outlines the changes that need to be made before a child can return to the birth home. Items within the plan pinpoint behaviors and situations that contributed to child being removed from the birth home, as well as the required steps taken to make sure maltreatment does not happen again.

Typically, birth parents have about a year to prove to CPS, and a child welfare judge, that they have met all the plan's requirements and the child should be returned to their care. Hearings to determine if a permanency plan has been created and worked toward must be held twelve months after a child has been removed and placed in foster care. Sometimes the permanency hearing can be postponed for another six months, if good reason to do so is shown. Reviews are heard in juvenile or family court every six months while a child is in foster care, to make sure progress is being made toward helping the child achieve permanency.

The hope is that the child is reunited with the birth family and that he or she will remain there, safe and well cared for, on a permanent basis. If birth parents either cannot or will not meet the goals of a permanency plan in the time allowed, then CPS and the courts begin looking at other permanent living situations for foster children. Adoption could be an option in this case. A termination of parental rights hearing determines when and if the child is available for adoption.

CHAPTER THREE

Issues and Outlooks

Foster care in the United States is an attempt to keep vulnerable children safe and families together. However, good intentions are not always enough. A system this important needs a full range of resources to make sure it meets expectations and can accomplish its goals. It also should be monitored and reviewed from time to time, to make sure it is working properly and serving the needs of everyone it aims to help.

Making sure the US foster care system is adequately funded and staffed requires federal and state legislation. Enacting and amending laws can be a part of foster care reform, which is aimed at keeping the system up-to-date, on track, and true to its goals. In the case of reform, legislation shines a spotlight on trouble spots within the system even as it attempts to correct them.

Running foster care in the United States involves lots of paperwork. Some of it comes in the form of legislation designed to make the system work better and address problems.

Socially Secure Children and Families

In the United States, the term "Social Security" is most closely linked with benefits the elderly receive once they are no longer working. But

Foster Care Bill of Rights

In 1973, Philadelphia's Independence Hall—the same place where the Declaration of Independence and the United States Constitution were adopted—played host to another historic event: the signing of the nation's first Bill of Rights for Foster Children.

Similar to the Constitution's Bill of Rights, this new document detailed several undeniable rights owed to every child placed in foster care. These included rights every child, whether or not he or she is in the foster care system, should have (the rights to an education, to reach their full potential, and to be part of a family and loved). But other rights were included that reflected the unique situation of foster children (the rights to receive help in overcoming abuse/neglect, to legal representation during foster care hearings, to receive quality childcare services, and to take part in decisions that will affect them for the rest of their lives).

As of 2019, twenty-six states have established their own versions of a foster care bill of rights, either as a matter of public policy or as an actual law on the state books. Newer versions often include the right of foster kids to be told why they are in foster care and where they stand in the process.

these benefits are only part of the story. When the Social Security Act was passed in 1935, the intent of the law was meant to protect the general welfare of the American public. Programs were established to help not only the elderly but the poor and disabled as well.

In 1962, amendments were added to the Social Security Act that gave the states federal money to create and manage child protection programs as part of their social service and welfare offerings. In order to get the money, states had to develop a plan detailing how children would be cared for while in the foster system, as well as ways to improve a child's home life so that he or she could either rejoin the birth family or be placed with a relative. This seems to be an early version of permanency planning, which is required in today's foster care system.

Then Came CAPTA

The Child Abuse Prevention and Treatment Act (CAPTA) was passed in 1974. Considered by many to be the granddaddy of child welfare legislation, CAPTA spelled out exactly what the role of the states was with regard to child welfare. It also expanded the level of assistance they could receive from the federal government. Under the terms of CAPTA, federal money was to be used to:

- Investigate reports of maltreatment
- Assess family situations and risks to children in the birth home
- Offer treatment services to address abusive and neglectful behavior

Those accused of abuse can be prosecuted using federal money, thanks in part to the early US child protection legislation known as CAPTA.

- Prosecute serious offenders
- Prevent cases of maltreatment from getting worse or happening in the first place

Definitions of what should be considered abuse or neglect were also included in the act. In addition, CAPTA emphasized the need for research on topics related to foster care and child welfare policy, such as education and training for mandatory reporters and data collection for cases of abuse and neglect. A set of standards for evaluating state-run child welfare agencies also was a point of consideration under this legislation.

CAPTA is reviewed and reauthorized on a regular basis. With each reauthorization, the states must adopt new rules and regulations to meet CAPTA requirements.

Placement and Permanence Legislation

Six years after CAPTA was made law, the Adoption Assistance and Child Welfare Act of 1980 attempted to tackle the issues of foster child placement and permanency. The latter act directed CPS caseworkers to do everything possible in order to avoid unnecessarily removing children from their birth homes and families. If removal

Federal law has urged placing foster kids in private homes rather than government detention centers, which have been used to house immigrant families, such as these in Texas.

was necessary, then the preferred setting should be a family foster home or smaller private and public childcare institutions. The act stated that detention centers and public group homes that housed more than twenty-five children were ineligible to receive federal funds to support foster care placements.

As its name states, the Adoption Assistance and Child Welfare Act also offered states financial adoption assistance for eligible children who had been in the foster care system. Eligibility depended upon the "special needs" of children, meaning circumstances that could reasonably be expected to harm the child's chances of being adopted without the incentive of extra financial help provided to the adoptive family. Special needs children under the act included, but were not limited to:

- Teens and/or older kids
- Siblings who were placed together
- Children of certain ethnicities
- Children with certain medical conditions

Too Long, Too Many, Not Enough

Some of the most common complaints about foster care in the United States revolve around the idea that many children seem to be stuck in the system for long periods of time, and therefore face being placed in multiple foster homes while they are in the system. The federal government tried to ease these situations with the passage of the Adoption and Safe Families Act (ASFA). Various provisions of the act encourage cutting through red tape so that children are not in the system for too long, which also means there is less chance of them being shuttled from one placement to another as the process continues.

Enacted in 1997, ASFA required caseworkers to put together a permanency plan for foster children as soon as possible, while keeping in mind that concerns about child safety came first. The act gave state CPS offices the power to file additional permanency plans at the same time it develops reunification plans. This way, if the preferred birth family reunification did not take place in the time allowed, the state would not need to waste time writing up a new permanency plan that centered on permanent placement with a relative or adoption. Also important was the requirement that, except in certain circumstances, states must file termination of parental rights requests as soon as kids have been in the system for a total of fifteen out of the previous twenty-two months. Finally, the act clearly states that preference should be given to relatives when placing foster children.

Legislation aimed at helping foster kids get a jump-start on achieving independence once they "aged out" of the system was enacted in 1999. The Foster Care Independence Act enhanced and expanded services available to current and former foster teens in order to help them become self-sufficient. Independence readiness is a huge issue in foster care. Many experts claim that, traditionally, there have not been enough programs available to prepare foster teens for life on their own when they leave the foster care system (at age eighteen or twenty-one, depending on the state). Included in the Foster Care Independence Act are provisions that help states provide training and education opportunities, counseling services, help finding a place to live, and other programs/assistance for this group of older foster kids.

Flanked by foster teens, former US president Bill Clinton signs the Foster Care Independence Act, designed to help those leaving the system to live independently.

Keeping Track of the Trafficked

It is a sad fact that all too often, kids in the foster care system become the targets of human traffickers. Researchers estimate that up to 60 percent of the one hundred thousand or so child sex trafficking victims in the United States have been in the child welfare system at one time or another. Having had an unstable home life and experiencing abuse are two contributing factors that make foster kids vulnerable to entering this illegal trade. Teens who run away from an unhappy or difficult foster home, and those who feel lost after aging out of the system, account for a number of sex-trafficking victims as well.

In an attempt to keep current and former foster kids safe from trafficking, the federal government signed into law the Preventing Sex Trafficking and

An Ounce of Prevention

As a way to lower the number of children removed from their homes and placed in foster care, the US Congress passed a bill in 2018 that emphasized providing in-home services to troubled families across the country. The Family First Prevention Services Act (FFPSA) calls for a portion of child welfare funding to be put toward prevention programs, rather than placements outside the home or adoptions.

Under the act, birth parents would have access to support services early on, in the hope that they can solve their problems before the situation gets to the point where CPS recommends child removal. Support services include substance abuse rehabilitation, mental health counseling, and parenting skills education. Also included in the FFPSA were measures that limited the amount of time children spent in group foster homes and cuts in funding to group settings.

Strengthening Families Act of 2014. The law requires states to identify foster children who are potential or actual victims of sex trafficking and develop plans for serving these at-risk youths. Chief among the provisions of the law is the requirement to report such cases immediately. It is hoped that knowing what factors may have led foster kids to the sex trade will help legislators and child health workers find ways to prevent more children and teens from becoming trafficking statistics. Also, it is believed that reporting such cases gives law enforcement and CPS a better chance of locating and helping victims of human trafficking who are in the system.

States Taking the Lead

When it comes to legislation regarding foster children and teens, states usually follow the lead of the federal government—writing, adding to, or otherwise changing state laws to sync with federal ones so that they meet requirements linked to child welfare funding. Occasionally, however, states have been known to take matters into their own hands and pass laws and statutes that benefit foster kids and their families. Such was the case in 2018 when the California legislature and Governor Jerry Brown passed Assembly Bill 2119, which gives

Former California governor Jerry Brown took the lead in pushing through legislation that benefited transgender foster teens in his state.

transgender teens in the foster care system access to gender-affirming medical care.

Under prior state child welfare law, transgender foster youths in California were able to receive hormone and surgical treatments if they were deemed "medically necessary." What the new law does is more clearly define such treatments, as well as mental health counseling, as rights that should not be denied to transgender foster youths. The law also gives these individuals greater say in what goes into their case plans, including access to gender-affirming treatments.

Minors in California's foster care system still need to receive consent from a parent, a caseworker, licensed caregiver, or judge before undergoing gender-affirming medical or surgical treatment.

Also in 2018, the Virginia General Assembly passed a bill

that lets the commonwealth's foster teens weigh in on whether or not the parental rights of their birth parents should be reinstated. At foster care review hearings, foster kids ages fourteen and older who have been placed in a permanent foster care setting or are preparing to live independently may ask a judge, through a lawyer or court-appointed representative, to give parental rights back to the people accused of mistreating them. The judge is then required to open up an investigation to determine if the teen would be safe back in the birth family home.

Myths & FACTS

Myth: Kids, especially teens, wind up in foster care because they are juvenile delinquents.

Fact: Children and teens are placed in foster care in an attempt to keep them safe from a bad or dangerous home environment. Except in a few rare instances, foster kids are in the system through no fault of their own.

Myth: Because there is a shortage of foster homes, a lot of kids end up in group homes or some other kind of institution.

Fact: While many states report difficulty finding foster parents willing to take kids into their homes, data shows that the majority of kids in foster care are placed in private homes (45 percent) or with relatives (32 percent).

Myth: Once children are removed from their homes, they stop having contact with their birth parents.

Fact: Nearly half of all children in the foster care system are reunified with their birth parents. Also, during a foster care placement, communication and visits between children and their birth parents are encouraged and made possible.

CHAPTER FOUR

Challenges Foster Children May Face

The reason foster care exists is to keep children and teens safe. Maltreatment, in its many forms, is harmful to children, and studies have shown that the negative effects of abuse and neglect can be long lasting. In other words, abuse and neglect can follow children and teens for years. With regard to child welfare and the foster care system, solutions to this problem are to stop the maltreatment from occurring and/or somehow remove the victim from the source of the trouble, meaning remove the child from the birth home.

Unfortunately, CPS involvement and foster placement may not keep children and teens safe from all harm. Participation in the system—which includes being removed from one's home and living elsewhere for an unknown length of time—

Homelessness is just one of several issues that can stick with children who have been abused or neglected long after their mistreatment and/or their time in foster care.

comes with its own problematic side effects. So in addition to the lasting effects of the maltreatment, foster kids may also face challenges created by being in foster care itself. These challenges may be physical, emotional, or social in nature. Often there is crossover, where one type of maltreatment can result in challenges in multiple categories.

Body of Evidence

When discussing the physical challenges caused by maltreatment, most people would automatically think of bumps, bruises, and breaks that may be the result of abuse. Cases of physical harm that can be seen on the body of a child or teen are classic telltale signs that abuse has occurred. In fact, marks on a person are one of the factors that may cause people to report a family to CPS in the first place, especially mandated reporters such as doctors and others in the medical field. Recording the occurrence of visible injuries, either in writing or using images, may later help child welfare or law enforcement investigators prove that abuse has occurred.

Neglect can also cause physical harm. Not getting enough to eat, or receiving poor nutrition from whatever food is provided, can lead to several problems in this area. Low weight, stunted growth, and loss or weakening of muscle are examples

When Fostering Goes Bad

In general, foster children, particularly those living with relatives or in private homes with foster parents, are safe from abuse and neglect. This does not mean that physical harm cannot, and does not, happen while a person is in foster care. There have been instances where foster parents and relatives take out their frustrations and stress on the child or teen, especially when they are not properly trained or ready to handle life with a child who has been mistreated. People who do not take their role in the system seriously, who do not genuinely care, also have the potential for abuse or neglect.

Some people agree to take in foster children for all the wrong reasons, including family guilt or trying to impress others. As caregivers, foster parents are paid by the state to cover each foster child's expenses; most states also provide an allowance for things like clothing and school supplies. There have been reported cases of foster parents misusing child welfare funds. Other foster parents have been accused of taking a page from history—when foster children were used as laborers in exchange

Teenage boys are known for their huge appetites. But sometimes children in homes where neglect occurs don't have the option of raiding the fridge, and they wind up malnourished.

for room and board—and trying to get cheap/free babysitting or cleaning services.

Finally, some experts say that there is a greater likelihood of maltreatment in group homes than with kinship or private-home placements. Cases of threats, fights, beatings, and sexual abuse at the hands of group-home staff and other foster youths have been reported.

of physical issues that result from malnutrition. Children who do not eat proper amounts of healthy foods also may get sick more often and take longer to heal after illness or injury. Some studies have tried to show a link between weight gain/obesity and maltreatment, most likely caused by stress eating or eating a lot of junk food, but nothing has been proven in this area.

Getting Attached

Just as they may leave physical marks, childhood maltreatment can leave emotional scars. Obviously, being hurt or ignored by people who are supposed to love and protect them obviously makes a lasting impression on children and teens who are abused and neglected. Such a situation is likely to create trust issues, where foster kids have trouble believing they can rely on adults for anything, especially when it comes to keeping them safe. Being hurt and mistreated also can damage children's self-esteem. They may believe they are unworthy of love and attention, since these things were not given freely, if at all, by their birth parents.

As part of normal human development, children get attached to the adults who play an important role in their lives. Chief among these are parents, whom children look to for guidance

Scheduled time with members of their extended family can go a long way toward helping kids cope with being in foster care.

and care. When young children are removed from their birth homes and separated from their parents, they often experience what is known as separation anxiety. They feel awfully uncomfortable to downright fearful, worrying that they may never feel that special (and necessary) connection again, with their parents or anyone new.

One way to help cope with separation anxiety is for the foster child to have regular contact with their birth parents, when appropriate. Since about half of all foster care cases in the United States have reunification as their permanency plan goal, it stands to reason that, in at least those cases, parent-and-child visits would not only be allowed, but encouraged. Foster parents and birth parents also may work together toward permanency. Efforts such as these help foster children maintain old attachments with the birth family while developing new one with the foster family.

Trauma Wards

The name for a person's response to events that are deeply upsetting is trauma. Studies have shown that wards of the state are at great risk of being traumatized. Abuse and neglect fall into this category. So, too, do some of the events that foster children experience while they are in foster care. For instance, the act of being removed from his or her home is bound to be a traumatic experience for any child. Separation from birth parents and siblings; being in a new neighborhood or school because of a foster care placement; multiple placements within the system; and trying to reunite with one's birth family after time away also may be very upsetting.

Scientists believe that trauma created by maltreatment or navigating the foster care system can result in post-traumatic stress disorder (PTSD) in some children. Normally associated with soldiers who have been to war, PTSD can include symptoms such as depression, anger, trouble sleeping, and repeated dreams or memories about traumatic events. Not every foster child develops PTSD, but it reportedly is quite common. A 2005 study conducted by Harvard Medical School determined that children who had been in the foster care system were more likely to suffer from PTSD than US military veterans.

Making sure that foster kids receive counseling is an important step when dealing with trauma and PTSD. Foster parents and other adults who are willing to listen are a great help as well. Foster children and teens can help themselves by discovering their triggers, which are actions and situations that make people with PTSD relive the trauma. The idea behind recognizing their triggers is for them to either avoid or better prepare for such events when possible.

Social Issues

When it comes to social factors, the outlook for kids who have been in the foster care system is not great. A number of surveys, studies, and government reports on teens who have aged out of the system show that former foster kids are at higher risk for negative outcomes than those who had never entered foster care. Areas of concern include education issues, unemployment, and homelessness.

Education

The highly regarded, multiyear and multistate Chapin Hall Midwest Study measures how young

Certain studies have suggested that many foster kids struggle to perform well, get good grades, and stay in school.

adults function within society after they are no longer in the child welfare system. One of the top factors the study considers is how much schooling former foster kids receive. In general, former foster kids reported having a tougher time in school. Study authors found that children and teens in foster care were more likely to repeat a grade than young adults in general and were twice as likely to not even finish high school. They considered that changing schools because of foster placement(s) could be a major reason for being held back and receiving poor grades in general. Likewise, behavior issues—possibly linked to trauma or frustration at doing poorly in school—that resulted in suspension or expulsion could be blamed for foster children and teens not receiving a diploma.

Unemployment

Not finishing high school or college contributes to poor outcomes regarding employment. Those who age out of foster care are more likely to be unemployed or underemployed (earning very little) than other young adults in their age group. In fact, the Chapin Hall Midwest Study puts the unemployment rate among former foster youth at close to 50 percent. Several studies conducted from the 1980s through to the recent past back up these findings, stating that former foster children are more likely than young adults their same age to:

- Earn wages low enough to put them at the poverty level
- Not earn enough cash to live independently
- Take part in federal programs that provide financial assistance

A national foundation aimed at foster care reform, the Casey Family Programs released data in 2005 showing that slightly more than 80 percent of former foster children participating in the foundation's Northwest Foster Care Alumni Study had managed to land jobs. However, the report also concluded that general-population kids in the same age group as those surveyed typically had an employment rate of 95 percent. More-recent studies show that former foster youths still lag behind young adults who have never been in the foster system when it comes to employment.

Homelessness

According to a report issued by the National Alliance to End Homelessness, about one-quarter of all young adults who had been in foster care admitted that they had been homeless sometime during the

Experts agree that measures need to be taken so that former foster youths do not wind up homeless and in need of help from institutions such as food kitchens.

first few years of independence from the system. That number could double for teens formerly in the foster system if they also had a history as a juvenile offender before leaving foster care. Other strikes against former foster youths, such as going through multiple placements or having been the victim of physical abuse while still within the system, also increase the odds of homelessness once living independently.

Getting an Extension

Foster children and teens should not get discouraged about the challenges they may face as a result of their time in the system. First, each foster's experience is different. The number, frequency, and intensity of problems faced are going to be different from person to person. With counseling and other assistance, foster youths are better equipped to deal with whatever outcomes they may meet along the way.

Second, times change, and so do the terms under which the child welfare system is run. Reform efforts, at the state and federal level, bring about changes designed to help the system better serve the children and families in its care. Foster care extension programs are examples of successful child welfare reform measures. As studies detailing possible challenges seem to confirm, teens frequently are unprepared for independent living after they age out of the system. By giving teens the option of extending their time in or returning to foster care, states and the federal government have made transitioning from protective care to independent living much easier. In addition to receiving foster care services, particularly financial assistance, teens in extended care programs also may receive independent-living skills training.

In order to take part in these programs, foster teens must meet certain requirements. These include working toward a high school diploma, vocational school certificate, or college degree; receiving job training; or working part-time while going to school or trying to secure full-time employment. Caseworkers sign off on a teen's need for extended foster care and also help determine when the teen is ready to make it on his or her own.

CHAPTER FIVE

Coping Mechanisms

Foster care is one of those situations where, in order for it to work, people have to take the bad with the good. The promise of protection and a chance to change the way family members treat each other are on the good side of the system. On the negative side is being removed from one's home and placed in an unfamiliar situation, facing new challenges—and, if the placement is a bad match for any reason, possibly facing a few old challenges.

The unpleasant and traumatic factors associated with the US foster care system will never totally go away. Fortunately, foster children and teens have the ability to "take the edge off" any negative experiences by finding and using a variety of coping mechanisms. These actions, habits, and processes can help foster kids deal with

Meditation is an option for kids and teens looking to relieve the stress associated with being in the foster care system. (Foster parents might want to partake in meditation as well!)

their situation in a way that gives them more control over their own minds, bodies, and spirits.

Pay Attention

It is easy for children and teens to get caught up in the many changes that take place during the whole foster care experience. Unfortunately, when that happens, the very people who are supposed to benefit from all the commotion can get lost in the shuffle. Foster kids and their well-being are still the center of attention, but what about the kids they were before the maltreatment, removal, and child welfare placement? How do they manage the day-to-day stuff—going to school, hanging out with friends, having a part-time job, and more—when they are busy dealing with being in foster care?

Taking advantage of a few time-tested self-help tricks could be important in this situation. The first is mindfulness, a word used to describe focusing only on the present moment. In practice, this involves foster kids noticing what is going on around them right then and there, and not focusing on their troubled pasts or uncertain futures. Being mindful benefits foster children and teens because it helps them stay calm and make smart decisions.

Self-awareness means paying careful attention to everything about oneself, honestly and without judgment. It's a bit like putting together a jigsaw puzzle, where a bunch of smaller pieces come together to form a whole person. Thoughts, feelings, likes, dislikes, strengths, weaknesses, and the reasons why people do what they do should all be taken into account on the road to becoming self-aware.

Foster youths can be extra hard on themselves, thinking there must be something wrong with them because they were removed from their homes and their living situation is so different from that of "regular" kids. Perhaps they even blame themselves for being in the system. Self-awareness can help turn that around. There is strength in foster youths understanding themselves as completely as possible, and consequently being much more comfortable in their own skin.

See and Be Seen, Hear and Be Heard

For older kids and teens in the foster care system, self-awareness should go beyond taking stock of certain personal characteristics. These individuals should also make a point of knowing where they stand in the foster care process, from start to finish. More than that, they should be contributing members of their own foster care experience.

First and foremost, foster children and teens have the right to be told why they have been removed from their homes and placed in foster care. This information should come from the child welfare caseworker assigned to the case or the lawyer representing the child in court. Individuals should feel free to ask a CPS or court-appointed representative for this information if it is not readily mentioned.

Contributing to their permanency plans is an important step toward foster children staying up-to-date with where their individual cases are within the foster care system. Foster kids who are self-aware and informed about the reasons for their removal are in a better position to communicate their wants and needs through their child welfare permanency plan. In fact, involving foster teens in their case planning is such an important part of the process that, in 2014, the United States government lowered the age at which participation is required from sixteen to fourteen.

Kids in the foster care system also are encouraged to attend legal hearings related to their case. Not only will older children and teens be able to uncover information about their cases, but this is another situation in which they may be able to explain for themselves what happened before removal, tell the judge how they are doing in their foster placement, and give input as to what they would like to see happen with regard to permanency. Younger children may be asked simple questions, but older kids generally get the most benefit from attending hearings.

Each of these steps toward being seen and heard accomplishes two important goals. One, they remind everyone that there is a real, live person at the center of the process who needs help living a safe and happy life. Two, the steps give foster kids a certain feeling of satisfaction, knowing that they didn't remain

Hitting a ball, riding a bike, or simply walking around the block can "take the edge off" when someone is dealing with issues surrounding foster care.

ignorant, silent, or helpless while everyone else was making decisions about them and for them.

Paths Toward Emotional Coping

When negative feelings and events occur, it can often seem as if they are threatening to take over a person's

Eat, Drink, Exercise, and Be Merry

While they are being helped by others, foster youths can look out for their own well-being by taking care of themselves through diet and exercise. That may seem like an overly simple thing to mention, but eating right and getting active actually have a number of benefits, especially for handling emotional upsets.

Think of diet and exercise as a way to put someone's mind at ease. Scientists have proven that exercise releases serotonin, a "feel-good" chemical, into a person's brain. While this chemical can't completely take away depression and anxiety, it can certainly lift the spirits of someone suffering from these emotions.

Malnutrition from not eating nutritious food is one example of maltreatment that can get a child or teen removed from his or her birth home. It makes sense, then, that it's not a good idea for foster kids, especially those with emotional issues, to eat a lot of junk food. Eating well helps keep a person strong and healthy, which can make dealing with the tough times a little easier.

life completely. The thing to remember is that, as with most foster care placements themselves, the bad stuff is usually only temporary. Until the fear and anxiety pass, there are a number of techniques that help children and teens deal with the emotional fallout associated with foster care.

Unlike self-awareness, which involves looking deep inside oneself, many methods of emotional coping center on foster youths getting "outside their own heads" for a while. This is accomplished mainly by sharing and venting. Sharing is another way of saying foster youths can talk about their experiences and concerns with someone they trust. Venting is just as it sounds—a chance to let off steam! Both methods are a great way to handle stress, anger, and depression.

CPS caseworkers and foster parents are required to arrange a meeting with a therapist or counselor at the request of the foster child or teen. But talking to someone about foster care issues, or anything that is concerning, does not have to be done in a formal, clinical setting. Discussing the situation with caseworkers and foster parents themselves should always be a safe option. If not, there are other people who make good sounding boards, including a number of adults who are mandated child welfare reporters, such as teachers. Simply talking with trusted friends is also a great option.

For foster kids and just about anyone, writing allows for self-expression in the moment, and a bit of introspection later on, as a way to see how things are going.

Foster kids who don't feel like talking might want to consider putting their thoughts and feelings in writing through journaling. One of the great things about writing in a diary or journal is that people can go back later and read what they have written. Being able to see how their feelings have, or haven't, changed over time can help foster children see if their situation is getting better or worse, or merely remaining the same. Then they can take any action they think is necessary based on what they discover. Another plus is that venting on paper definitely puts foster youths in a no-judgment zone, where they don't have to worry about how a listener is going to respond to what they have to say.

Act and Interact

Successfully dealing with being in foster care often involves finding ways to work within the existing child welfare system. Yet there is another method of coping, by changing the system as a reform advocate, which foster teens may find equally satisfying and effective.

An advocate is someone who gathers support for what he or she believes is a worthy cause. In the case of child welfare reform advocacy, the worthy cause is making foster care better for those who go through the system. Children and teens who are or have been foster youths have first-hand experience with the system and therefore can give special insights into how it might be improved. They can present their ideas in a number of ways, including, but not limited to:

- Getting signatures for a petition to be sent to local or state lawmakers, who are responsible

Talking about important issues, and getting feedback from others about those issues, are key elements when becoming an advocate for a cause.

for proposing and passing child-welfare legislation

- Writing letters to politicians and child welfare officials, urging them to consider making changes to the system
- Fund-raising for the local chapter of a child welfare group
- Posting comments on social media about the foster care experience
- Organizing information events on child protection, foster care, and adoption
- Organizing or participating in protests

Teens should make every effort to be well-behaved and on the right side of the law while performing advocacy work.

On a more personal level, teens in the system might consider volunteering with a group that serves foster kids such as themselves. Organizations such as Boys Town and Together We Rise provide outreach to foster children and would probably be very happy to have volunteers pitch in for the cause.

10 Great Questions to Ask a Social Worker

1. Why was I taken out of my home and placed in foster care?
2. Have you been able to find any relatives willing to take care of me?
3. Is there an available foster home near my birth home/neighborhood/school?
4. When is my next hearing scheduled?
5. How often will I be able to visit with my birth family?
6. Whom do I contact if an issue comes up with my foster parents?
7. Will you help me find a counselor or therapist to talk to?
8. What will happen to me if I can't go back to my birth family?
9. What programs should I take part in to help me live independently?
10. What can I do to make this process go smoother and faster?

CHAPTER SIX

Here to Help

No one should have to navigate through the child welfare system, or cope with being placed in foster care, alone. Dealing with just about any stressful situation is made better when a person knows he or she has a support system to help along the way. Thankfully, there are individuals and groups who can help. Some, such as caseworkers and GALs, are built in to the system—individuals who are mandated by state or federal law to provide assistance to foster youths and their families. Others are volunteers who, for personal reasons, offer to assist because they take an interest in and care about foster youth in their community. Then there are the people who help because they were once foster kids themselves.

Spending time with someone who is willing to listen and help is a great way to cope with being in foster care.

On the Case

Among the first people foster children should turn to when they have questions or need information about their situation should be their caseworker. Possibly due to their role in removing children and teens from their birth homes, caseworkers may be thought of as less than helpful in foster care matters. It is important to consider, however, that removal and placement are just a small part of their responsibilities. The main thrust of their work as Child Protective Services agents is to protect vulnerable kids and, except in extreme cases of maltreatment, bring families back together, safely, under one roof.

Caseworkers' in-depth knowledge of the system in which they work enables them to help foster children and teens cope. They know the rules and regulations surrounding child welfare and can advise foster children and families regarding what needs to be done and when. Some of the stress associated with being in foster care has to do with not feeling informed or in control. Caseworkers can help give foster kids back a certain amount of control by managing the many elements of the foster care process, especially when it comes to court hearings and the creation of a permanency plan. Building a good relationship with their caseworker gives foster kids the best chance to help themselves while they are in the care of the state.

Filling the Parental Void

Foster parents are individuals who offer to care for foster kids in their homes. That means making

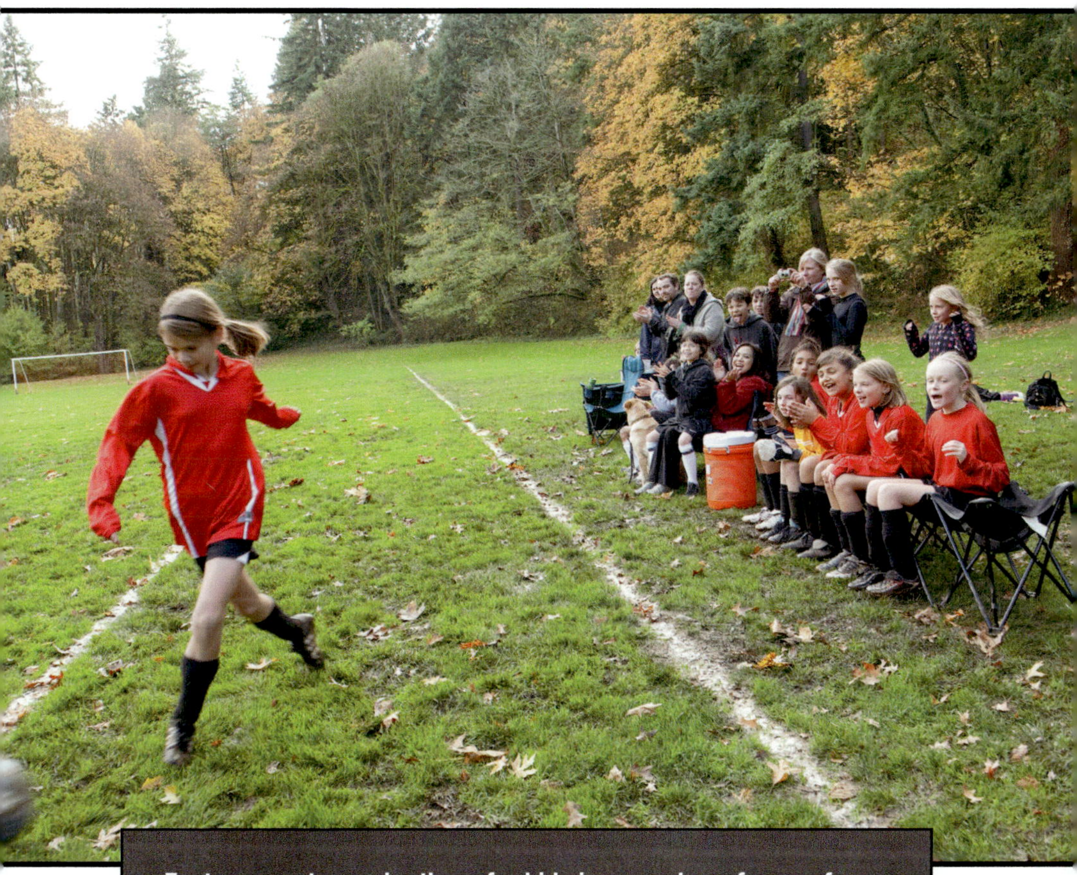

Foster parents can be there for kids in a number of ways, from cheering on the sidelines of a soccer game to listening as a foster child vents about his or her situation.

sure children are fed, clothed, go to school, and are safe—basically the same things birth parents should do—until a permanent home for the child can be found. This can include placing the foster child back with the birth family, with an adoptive family, or with the foster parents themselves, if they are able and willing to adopt their foster child.

The very nature of their role in the lives of foster children and teens makes foster parents a source of help. In addition to material things, foster parents give kids time and attention. Another part of the job description for foster parenting is being a good communicator. That not only means foster parents can give kids advice, but they also know they need to be good listeners.

People receive training before becoming foster parents, so they know what they are supposed to do, as well as how to handle tough situations. In particular, their training covers how to help someone deal with trauma in a sensitive, effective way. Screening is also part of the process for becoming a foster parent, so hopefully the people who take on the role of caregiver are good citizens with a decent background. Foster kids may get help from these caregivers simply by paying attention to what the adults say and do—in other words, treat them as role models.

Finally, foster parents are called upon to help foster children and teens keep a bond with their birth parents by arranging visits and phone calls. They may help birth parents in other ways, such as helping them form permanency plans or simply chatting with them about the hurdles they face being a parent. Helping with the reunification of birth families is one more way foster parents can help kids get through being in the foster care system.

Sure, not every foster placement is a raging success. Sometimes foster parents mean well but have trouble bonding with their foster children—kind of like what happens all the time between

Coordinated Help

The courtroom is not the only place where foster kids can find individuals whose mission is to give them specialized, dedicated help. Foster youths preparing to leave the child welfare system and live on their own can get a little extra assistance when they most need it through an independent living program, or ILP. Funded by the states or the federal government, ILPs provide life skills such as money management and interviewing for a job. Federally funded education and training voucher (ETV) programs give financial assistance to foster kids who have either aged out of the system or who live with a relative who has agreed to be their legal guardian. Both ILPs and ETVs employ coordinators whose job it is to work one-on-one with young adults to help them obtain needed services covered by these programs.

Learning how to do well in interviews is just one of the life skills taught via an independent living program. It can help you land a job and build a successful career.

children and their birth parents. By giving these adults the benefit of the doubt, and doing their part toward making the placement a success, foster children and teens stand a very good chance of getting tons of help from their foster parents.

That's My GAL

During court hearings, those in the foster care system can benefit greatly from the efforts of a guardian ad litem (GAL). This professional is appointed by the court to look out for the best interest of a minor, who is someone younger than eighteen. GALs do not need to have a law degree, although some do. Whether or not a GAL is a lawyer, he or she has legal standing in court to speak and act on behalf of minor foster children. In many states, GALs are paid a small amount (not close to what an attorney makes), with their fees most likely paid by the child's parents.

Essentially, GALs are legal representatives appointed to act and speak on the behalf of minor children in court. In order to do their job to the best of their ability, they launch investigations into reports of abuse and neglect, interview witnesses, hold birth parents accountable for working on a permanency plan and meeting any other court-

Been There, Done That

Groups of people who have been through similar troubles may find comfort in coming together and sharing their experiences. That is the principle behind support groups such as Alcoholics Anonymous. In fact, being free to express oneself without having to explain anything or feel embarrassed is actually a relief for many.

A quick internet search reveals several support groups for foster parents, but not as many for children and teens who are currently in foster care. More common are support groups for older foster youths and those who have aged out of the system, such as the peer support program run by Foster Care Alumni of America.

ordered requirements, and explain legal proceedings to those they represent. Unlike lawyers, GALs can act as witnesses on behalf of their clients.

Only those age twenty-one or older are allowed to be GALs. The typical requirements to become a

Gathering to share their foster care experiences with people who also have been in the system can give kids the support they need as they work to live independently.

GAL include passing a federal background check and participating in training courses that take about thirty hours to complete.

Foster children and teens should never underestimate the helping power of volunteers either. Court appointed special advocates (CASAs) go through the same training and perform many of the same duties as a GAL, but they do so on their own time, free of charge. Those duties include reviewing a foster child's case and presenting their findings, verbally or in writing, before the judge. They give the court progress reports on foster care placements and permanency plans, and talk to children about their cases, making sure that kids understand, to the best of their ability, what's happening from a legal angle.

(Role) Model Behavior

Sometimes getting assistance with legal issues and paperwork just isn't enough. Foster children and teens also might appreciate help on a more personal level—help simply finding out more about who

Mentors don't just give advice or help their mentees get over rough spots. They also make time to take part in fun activities and enjoy the company of their mentees.

they are or want to be. Sometimes, they need a mentor.

Mentoring programs are run by child welfare organizations and nonprofits that serve young people. One of the most popular and well-known of these organizations is Big Brothers Big Sisters. When people volunteer to be mentors, they are interviewed, screened (through a background check), and trained to best connect with the children they mentor. Volunteers are matched with foster kids based on preferences (e.g., age and gender identity), interests, and similar principles.

Mentors are role models. Instead of trying to care for kids the way a birth or foster parent might, or trying to usher them through the child welfare system in some way, mentors participate in fun and interesting activities, such as going to a movie, playing games, taking on a special craft project, or even just chatting over a favorite snack. Their time together is regularly scheduled so that foster youths have something to look forward to and depend on at a time when there is so much uncertainty in their lives.

Experts believe that mentored youths make smarter life choices and are less likely to take part in risky behaviors, such as drug use or criminal activity. A 2009 study indicated that foster children and teens who had been mentored showed fewer signs of depression, were less stressed, and reported being happier, in general, than foster youths who have not. There are people who believe that this data goes to show that with a little help, reassurances that they are worthy of love and respect, and a lot of faith in themselves, foster children and teens can cope with whatever challenges come their way.

Glossary

abandonment The act of taking away one's protection and assistance.

ad litem Appointed by the court to represent a client in a particular legal action. Literally, "for the suit."

advocate To work toward supporting or promoting a cause.

burgeon To grow rapidly or flourish.

consent Legal permission or approval.

foster To take care of someone like a parent.

incapacitated No longer having the power to take care of someone or something.

kinship Having the same nature or being related.

malnutrition A medical condition that occurs when people do not eat enough food with a healthy amount of vitamins and minerals.

mandatory Required by law.

mentor One who teaches and guides, mainly by example and experience.

mindfulness The practice of being very aware and nonjudgmental about one's thoughts and feelings.

peer One who is at another person's equal level, socially and legally.

petition A formal, written request to investigate or take care of a matter; in child maltreatment cases, petitions are filed with a court.

placement Assigning a person to a location or physical space.

reform To change something with the goal of making it better.

reunification To bring back together after time apart.

substantiated Proved by evidence to be true.

terminate To bring to an end.

transition To move from one place or life stage to another.

vulnerable Capable of being easily attacked or hurt.

ward A person who is under the protection and care of another.

For More Information

Casey Family Programs

1123 23rd Avenue

Seattle, WA 98122-4821

(800) 496-2230

Website: http://www.casey.org

Facebook: @Casey.Family.Programs

Instagram: @caseyprograms

Twitter: @CaseyPrograms

Email: media@casey.org

YouTube: Casey Family Programs

Since 1966, Casey Family Programs has operated in every US state. The organization offers consulting, research, and data-collection services, as well as foster care advocacy.

Foster Care Alumni of America

5810 Kingstowne Center Drive, Suite 120-730

Arlington, VA 22315

(888) ALU-MNI0

Website: http://www.fostercarealumni.org

Facebook: @FCAANational

Twitter: @FCAANational

Email: info@fostercarealumni.org

The statewide chapters of Foster Care Alumni of America offer access to peer support, leadership training, and advocacy initiatives to former foster kids across the nation.

Foster Care to Success

23811 Chagrin Boulevard, Suite 210

Cleveland, OH 44122

(571) 203-0270

Website: http://fc2success.org

Facebook: @FosterCare2Success

Twitter: @FC2Success

YouTube: fc2success

Email: info@fc2success.org

Transitional services are Foster Care to Success's bread and butter. The organization helps foster teens prepare for independent living by offering education vouchers, academic mentoring, and scholarship opportunities.

FosterClub

620 S Holladay, Suite 1

Seaside, OR 97138

(503) 717-1552

Website: http://www.fosterclub.com

Facebook: @FosterClub

Instagram and Twitter: @fosterclub

YouTube: fosterclubTV

Email: info@fosterclub.com

FosterClub directly serves foster youths through training and education, peer support, advocacy, internships, and awards programs. Special programs address issues surrounding foster teens transitioning to independent living and offer support to caregivers.

Ontario Association of Children's Aid Societies (OACAS)

75 Front Street East, Suite 308

Toronto, ON M5E 1V9

Canada

(800) 718-1797

Website: http://www.oacas.org

Twitter: @our_children

Email: reception@oacas.org

As the lead organization of Children's Aid Societies throughout Canada, OACAS promotes the welfare of children, teens, and their families through leadership and advocacy efforts.

Youth in Care Canada

223 Main Street, Box 96

Ottawa, ON K1S 1C4

Canada

(800) 790-7074

Website: https://youthincare.ca

Facebook: @YouthInCareCanada

Instagram: Youth_In_Care_Canada

Twitter: @youthincare

Email: info@youthincare.ca

Youth in Care Canada aims to help those currently and formerly in the country's welfare system support and change that system. Offerings vary by province but include scholarship assistance and life-skills training.

Youth Law Center

832 Folsom Street, Suite 700

San Francisco, CA 94107

(415) 543-3379

Website: http://www.ylc.org

Facebook: @youthlawcenter

Twitter: @YouthLawCenter

Email: info@ylc.org

Advocating for foster medical, legal, and education support, as well as strengthening the family unit, the Youth Law Center supports initiatives focusing on parent education and training and independent-living success.

For Further Reading

Brown, Waln, and John Seita. *A Foster Care Manifesto: Designing the Alumni Movement.* Tallahassee, FL: William Gladden Foundation Publishing, 2013.

Langston-George, Rebecca. *Orphan Trains: Taking the Rails to a New Life.* Mankato, MN: Capstone Publishers, 2016.

Libal, Joyce. *The Foster Care System* (Living with a Special Need). Broomall, PA: Mason Crest, 2014.

McCormick, Adam. *LGBTQ Youth in Foster Care.* New York, NY: Routledge, 2018.

Shirk, Martha, and Gary Stangler. *On Their Own: What Happens to Kids When They Age Out of the Foster Care System.* New York, NY: Basic Books, 2006.

Sommers, Annie Leah. *Frequently Asked Questions About Foster Care.* New York, NY: Rosen Publishing Group, 2010.

Staley, Erin. *Defeating Stress and Anxiety.* New York, NY: Rosen Publishing Group, 2016.

Welsh, Elena. *Trauma Survivors' Strategies For Healing.* Emeryville, CA: Althea Press, 2018.

Woodson, Jacqueline. *Peace, Locomotion.* New York, NY: Puffin Books, 2010.

Bibliography

Adopt US Kids. "About the Children." Retrieved January 30, 2019. https://www.adoptuskids.org/meet-the-children/children-in-foster-care/about-the-children.

Chidea, Farai. "A Rare Foster Care Success Story." NPR News and Notes, December 4, 2006. https://www.npr.org/templates/story/story.php?storyId=6575906.

Child and Family Services Reviews. "Child Welfare Legislation." Retrieved February 23, 2019. https://training.cfsrportal.acf.hhs.gov/section-2-understanding-child-welfare-system/2992.

Children's Bureau. "The AFCARS Report." US Department of Health and Human Services, August 10, 2018. https://www.acf.hhs.gov/sites/default/files/cb/afcarsreport25.pdf.

Child Welfare Information Gateway. "CASAs and GALs." Children's Bureau. Retrieved February 2019. https://www.childwelfare.gov/topics/systemwide/courts/specialissues/casa-gal.

Child Welfare Information Gateway. "How the Child Welfare System Works." Children's Bureau, February 2013. https://www.childwelfare.gov/pubPDFs/cpswork.pdf#page=1&view=Introduction.

Child Welfare Information Gateway. "Major Federal Legislation Index and Search." Children's Bureau. Retrieved February 16, 2019. https://www.childwelfare.gov/topics/systemwide/laws-policies/federal/search/?CWIGFunctionsaction=federallegislation:main.getFedLedgDetail&id=22.

Child Welfare Information Gateway. "Overview: Courts." Children's Bureau. Retrieved February 16, 2019. https://www.childwelfare.gov/topics/systemwide/courts/overview.

Courtney, Mark E., et al. "Midwest Evaluation of the Adult Functioning of Former Foster Youth: Conditions of Youth Preparing to Leave State Care." Chapin Hall Center for Children at the University of Chicago, February 22, 2004. https://www.chapinhall.org/wp-content/uploads/Midwest-Study-Youth-Preparing-to-Leave-Care.pdf.

Degarmo, John. "Child Welfare Around the World." Fostering Families Today, September–October 2017. https://www.scribd.com/document/358171181/Child-Welfare-Around-the-World.

DePanfilis, Diane. "Child Protective Services: A Guide for Caseworkers 2018." Children's Bureau Office on Child Abuse and Neglect. Retrieved January 24, 2019. https://www.childwelfare.gov/pubPDFs/cps2018.pdf#page=6&view=Preface.

Haskins, Ron. "A National Campaign to Improve Foster Care." Brookings Institute, June 22, 2017. https://www.brookings.edu/research/a-national-campaign-to-improve-foster-care.

Pecora, Peter J., et al. "Improving Family Foster Care: Findings from the Northwest Foster Care Alumni Study." Casey Family Programs, March 14, 2005. https://caseyfamilypro-wpengine.netdna-ssl.com/media/AlumniStudies_NW_Report_FR.pdf.

Persall, Steve. "Tiffany Haddish Talks Growing Up in Foster Care and How She Learned to Be Herself in Comedy." *Tampa Bay Times*, August 30, 2017. http://www.tampabay.com/things-to-do/stage/tiffany-haddish-talks-growing-up-in-foster-care-and-how-she-learned-to-be/2335447.

Petersen, Anne C., et al., eds. "New Directions in Child Abuse and Neglect Research." National Academy of Sciences, March 25, 2014. https://www.ncbi.nlm.nih.gov/books/NBK195993.

Pokempner, Jenny, and Jennifer Rodriguez. "Foster Care in the United States: A Timeline." *Teen Vogue*, May 31, 2018. https://www.teenvogue.com/story/foster-care-in-the-united-states-a-timeline.

Reyes, Jill. "Child Welfare Bill of Rights for Foster Children." American Bar Association, January 9, 2018. https://www.americanbar.org/groups/child_law/resources/child_law_practiceonline/child_law_practice/vol_31/december_2012/child_welfare_billsofrightsforfosterchildren0.

Soulpancake. "I Survived Foster Care." YouTube, June 7, 2018. https://www.youtube.com/watch?v=0ezUEiwCFTg.

US House Ways and Means Committee. "Child Welfare Legislative History." United States House of Representatives. Retrieved February 5, 2019. https://greenbook-waysandmeans.house.gov/book/export/html/303.

Index

About the Author

A writer and editor living in Upstate New York, Jeanne Nagle has spent years researching and writing on topics that, like foster care, affect young adults and their families. Among her works are titles covering drug use and abuse, suicide, LGBTQ+ rights, and deportation.

Photo Credits

Cover Orange Line Media/Shutterstock.com; p. 5 Unique Nicole/Getty Images; p. 9 Jacob A. Riis/Archive Photos/Getty Images; p. 10 World History Archive/Newscom; pp. 14–15 Galleria Laureata/Shutterstock.com; p. 18 Helen H. Richardson/Denver Post/Getty Images; pp. 20–21 Florian Kopp/Alamy Stock Photo; p. 24 LaraBelova/iStock/Getty Images; p. 26 The Washington Post/Getty Images; p. 28 Rido/Shutterstock.com; p. 31 Thongchai S/Shutterstock.com; pp. 34–35 © AP Images; p. 39 Jetta Productions Inc/Digital Vision/Getty Images; p. 42 ftwitty/E+/Getty Images; pp. 44–45 John Moore/Getty Images; pp. 48–49 Tim Sloan/AFP/Getty Images; p. 52–53 Kevork Djansezian/Getty Images; p. 57 John Sommer/E+/Getty Images; p. 60 Image Source/Getty Images; p. 62 Thomas Barwick/Stone/Getty Images; p. 65 Syda Productions/Shutterstock.com; p. 68 New Africa/Shutterstock.com; p. 72 fizkes/Shutterstock.com; p. 76 Hill Street Studios/Digital Vision/Getty Images; p. 77 andresr/E+/Getty Images; p. 80 AnemStyle/Shutterstock.com; p. 82 Marc Romanelli/Getty Images; p. 85 PeopleImages/E+/Getty Images; p. 87 Yellow Dog Productions/Iconica/Getty Images; p. 90 sturti/E+/Getty Images; p. 93 Rawpixel.com/Shutterstock.com; pp. 94–95 MediaNews Group/Orange County Register/Getty Images.

Design: Michael Moy; Layout and Photo Researcher: Ellina Litmanovich; Editor: Erin Staley